The New York Survival Guide:
Don't Get Yourself Killed

By Trick Albright

Copyright © 2020 Nigel (Trick) Albright

ISBN: 9781657827011

All rights reserved

Introduction

Why did I write this book? To guide visitors and newcomers through this "third-rate Babylon," as H. L. Mencken called it. You will soon discover that folks from other civilized nations have the same difficulties with New York City and its denizens, as you will experience.

How to enjoy the Book

To help you take notice of important tips, facts, and minor exaggerations, take note of the following annotations used in the book. Each of these phrases are common to the New York metro and have the same meanings in this guide.

- **Not for nuttin'!** - Pay attention, for what follows is true.
- **Shut the Back Door!** - It's a true statement, but keep it to yourself.
- **Ya' Hump!** - Something every idiot knows.
- **Go Figure!** - Anything that's a mystery, often paradoxically so.
- **To Die For!** - It's good, no kidding!
- **Go Kill Yourself!** - It might be my opinion, prove me wrong!
- **Fuhgedaboudit!** - Funny Anecdote or Story.

Enjoy this guide as a regular front to back read and as a reference for coping with New Yorkers on your next visit. If you are already stuck here in this third-rate Babylon that is New York, this book may be just the lifeline you need to pull yourself from the morass, or at least off the suicide watch list.

Definition: Third World Country (noun): a country of extremes, widespread poverty, and with concentrated wealth. Minority groups are the predominant culture. Government policies are not aligned to America. (That sounds like New York all right.)

Preface

I'm an expatriated Southerner who came to New York to trade bonds on Wall Street and was completely unprepared for the Manhattan mayhem. I lived on the Upper East Side, Tribecca, and the Upper West Side. I've also lived in London and Holly Springs, MS. I've seen a lot and learned a lot about surviving in the urban landscape.

Over my fifteen-year sentence in NYC, I was often consulted by other expatriates on how to deal with the natives. Somehow people from other countries, without knowing much about Southerners or the British, realized that I was somehow different.

This guide will be different from other "coping with the natives" guides. No recipes from home. No moaning about beauty parlors or dry cleaners. And I'm not going to complain about vermin, noise, or bad smells. There will be, however, a list of common concerns from the civilized world so you know you're not alone.

For over 25 years, visitors from other countries have come to me for advice. As the song goes, "If you can make it there, you can make it anywhere." But it's up to this guide to help you to make it back again head-first—not feet-first.

Table of Contents

Introduction iii

How to enjoy the Book iii

Preface iv

Basic Communications 1

    The ubiquitous F-bomb. 3

What to Eat. 5

    The New York metro's contributions to cuisine: 7

    Know the sacred words for Pizza: 9

    The Classic Restaurants of New York 12

Greeting the Natives 15

    Catcall comebacks 19

Drink Until You Drop 21

    Befriending a Bartender Fast 22

    NYC Metro Liquor Laws 25

    Masterclass Drinking in NYC 27

    Hangover Cures for Pros 28

Conversation in New York 29

    NYC Terms and Vocabulary List 31

The Great Outdoors. 37

    Like golf? Tips to Get Tee-time 37

    Camping, Hiking, and, Hunger Games 38

Urban Camo	42
Avoiding Burial Expenses	44
Pro Tips for Blending In	44
Tipping	46
History of Tipping	46
Clever Ways to Avoid Tipping	49
If All Else False, How to Yank the Waiters Chain	50
Tip Amounts for All Services in NYC	51
FAQ Regarding Gratuities	52
Profile of the New Yorker	54
Here's what all the neighborhoods mean	55
Who Gets to Be a New Yorker?	57
New Yorker Street Cred	57
Protocols for the Largest Ethnic Groups	59
Chinese	59
Dominican	61
Indian	62
Russian	63
Afterword	67
About the Authors	68
Bibliography	69

The New York Survival Guide

Basic Communications

Incredibly, New York and Southern dialects have much in common. They are both the most widely recognizable of American dialects, and there is a widespread conviction that both groups punish the English language when spoken. While the South's drawl is attributed to the heat, New York accents are all about neighborhoods.

Not for Nuthin'! Linguists say the classic New York dialect is dying out—thanks to the sky-high price of living in Manhattan and the incessant droning of flat accented media from the Midwest.

One curious habit in New York is for every "r" that gets dropped, one gets added. It's called the intrusive "r." It's as if a New Yorker knew that they dropped the letter, so they put it in somewhere else in the same sentence. For example: "Get outta hea with yer idears." (Get out of here with your ideas).

Shut the Back Door! The letter "t" does not exist in the middle of words. Water is "wada"

Don't imitate the accents around the metro area. It won't fly. You might think you sound like Robert DeNiro in Taxi Driver ("you talkin' to me?"), but everyone listening hears Foghorn Leghorn. The New York accent is about a lot more than just dropping the r's and sticking them back in the wrong places. There's a whole vocabulary in just the copious gesticulations, not to mention the machine-gun interruptions. I find communicating with Yankees to be like trying to converse with someone riding a piano down a flight of stairs.

The New York Survival Guide

Not for Nuttin'! *In fact, the Metroplex dialect is so much about attitude and physicality that it even carries over to sign language. All the elements of the spoken accent are there: cursing, interrupting, and the occasional estranged "r."*

While the Southern accent sounds courteous, the British accent quaint, and the French accent, well, makes me want to disrobe—the New York accent suggests that person will pop a cap in your ass.

The metro area is regarded as forming its own subregion in terms of dialect variation in the United States. The mid-Atlantic was a melting pot of large-scale European immigration. New England and the South, on the other hand, were settled mainly by people from the British Isles. All this immigration variation has muddled the accents here so that they sound pretty much the same to outsiders—with one striking exception: the Locust Valley Lockjaw.

The Locust Valley Lockjaw: think Thurston Howe of *Gilligan's Island* or Jane Hathaway of *The Beverly Hillbillies*. Many folks find this accent rather pleasing. It's also fun and easy to imitate and will elevate your social status faster than "a frog shot out of a barn."

The accent is typically non-rhotic (a non-rhotic speaker drops the "r" sound) and involves speaking while keeping the lips tight and the jaw clenched and thrust forward with your neck extended. For practice, place a pencil crosswise just behind your eyeteeth and talk through it. Wouldn't hurt to download some *Gilligan's Island*.

Here's some of Thurston's best quotes for practice:

- "No one can pull the wool over my eyes. Cashmere maybe, but wool, never!"
- "If I can't go first class, I won't go at all."
- "Dash it all, Lovey, I've three-putted again."
- "I must dash down to Argentina to get a new string of polo ponies. It's just that I hate to ride a used polo pony."
- "Counting my money's made me sleepy."
- It is rather difficult being rich. If it wasn't for the money, I'd rather be poor."

The ubiquitous F-bomb.

Be aware that except in the case of the Locust Valley Lockjaw, you're going to hear the F-bomb. A lot. Don't fret, you will hear it so often you will soon be desensitized. The following is a rundown of common usage.

1. The word "fuck" can be used as a noun, verb, adjective, adverb, pronoun, or interjection and can logically be used as virtually any word in a sentence (e.g. "Fuck the fucking fucked-up fucked fuckers.")
2. "Fuck" is one of the few words in the English language which could be applied in the middle of a word. For example. "Am I sexy? Abso-fucking-lutely!"
3. "Fuck" is metaphorical. The verb "fucked" can mean "to be cheated" (e.g. "I got fucked by a plumber.") Unfortunately, this is not titillating unless the plumber was French—it means you just got charged $500 for a service call.

4. As a pronoun. "Hey ya' fuck." To describe a contemptible person as a "stupid fuck" or "dumb fuck." The verb "to fuck" may be used transitively or intransitively, and it appears in compounds, including "fuck off", "fuck up," and "fuck with."
5. The word can be used as an interjection and is sometimes used as a strong emphatic or in less explicit usage: "fuck" or "fuck with" can mean to bully or tease.
6. In a phrase such as "I don't give a fuck," the word is the equivalent of "damn," meaning "little regard of."
7. In "What the fuck," it serves as an intensive.
8. If something is very abnormal or FUBAR: "This is fucked up" may be said. Often you will hear the word repeated several times: "fuck-fuck-fuck-fuck" in singsong manner.
9. And finally, the affirmation: "Fucking A, B, and C!"

Not for Nuttin'! When you hear someone with a Locust Valley accent, politely offer to buy them a drink. It's your best chance of avoiding F-bombs. It's also your best bet for not getting mugged.

Shut the front door! You'll know you've been fully *desensitized when you've heard a tipsy grandmother scream, "Fuck you ref" at a Jets game and don't even flinch.*

Don't Get Yourself Killed! Hide your accent by gesticulations, high volume, and machine-gun interruptions. It's also about attitude. Fast, intense, and direct, no pleasantries. As long as you say it with conviction, you don't need to know what you're talking about.

What to Eat.

In Paris, you will enjoy a mélange of French food. Munich: a mishung of German food, Madrid a mezcla of Spanish food. New Orleans has rich creole. London has fish-n-chips, pudding and haggis. New York and metro have dough: pizza, bread, and pasta.

Shut the Back Door! Yeah, I know "haggis" is Scottish, but a list of three is more visually appealing and the Brits only have two dishes and one sauce. Note to the Brits—if you want to argue the point, take it up with Voltaire.

The New York Survival Guide

Why am I dragging the Brits into this? Because I lived in London, and, like London, the New York metro area has made few, arguably zero, palatable contributions to cuisine. The ethnic choices in the area, however, are tremendous. On any street you may find everything from pizza to pita, but mostly pizza. Manhattan is essentially a giant food court. It's crowded, noisy, and you're getting an American-ized knockoff of another culture's cuisine prepared by Guatemalans. Kidding? Hardly. Just check out the kitchen some time.

Go Kill Yourself! You might think I'm exaggerating about pizza, so my challenge to you is to find a "How to be a New Yorker" guide that doesn't mention pizza.

Go Figure! Pizza and Italian restaurants make up around 1/3 of restaurants in NYC, according to the data in the New York City Department of Health and Mental Hygiene. I know what your're thinking; I made that up. Sorry, but that's the real name. I would have called it something less outrageous like: "The NYC Department of Pissy Hands and Loonies."

To die for! Sonny's Famous Steaks in Philly. A review says: "The rolls are very soft, the beef juicier and more plentiful than most, the provolone nicely gooey, the Cheez Whiz well integrated into the meat." Cheez Whiz: the caviar of Philadelphia.

The New York Survival Guide

The New York metro's contributions to cuisine:

- New Jersey is responsible for three, sorry make that two, contributions to cuisine: grape juice and frozen food.
- Pennsylvania is regarded as the snack food capital of the world. Also renowned for pickles, ketchup, and, of course, the Philly Cheese Steak.
- New York has contributed hot dogs, cheesecake, and Manhattan Claim Crowder. By the way, even New Yorkers prefer the creamy New England Clam Chowder.
- Connecticut's contribution to cuisine is the hamburger, the white clam pizza, and—I am stretching to get three things in—the Subway franchise.

Grocery stores are small, even the largest ones. Forget about Publix, think more along the lines of a large 7-Eleven. No big deal? Probably not, you can order toilet paper through Amazon and have it drone delivered. What a sight that must be.

Go Kill Yourself! Food here is fantastically diverse varieties of wheat flour.

Go Figure! Don't be alarmed if you are shown a house with two kitchens; it's not a duplex. One kitchen is a "show kitchen" for display only. The other kitchen has not been used much either.

Not for Nuttin'! You may want to donate your taste-buds to science, because you won't be needing them here. But hey, you have pizza! And don't forget the other types of dough—both boiled and baked, sometimes both—that's a bagel.

In New York City, someone is going to push an "Egg Cream" on you. It's a beverage that has neither cream nor egg and consists of milk, soda water, and flavored syrup. It's not as bad as it sounds, and it's much better than...ah let me think......yeah, it's not really not better than anything.

To Die For! There are lots of great ethnic options in NYC. Look for a China Town, Little Italy, Koreatown, Little India, Greater Germany, etc.

Go Figure! Fine Dining in NYC is for the 1%. A meal at a top restaurant like Bâtard is approximately the same price as a plane ticket to another country where dough isn't the only thing on the menu. Bad news is that you'll need to call months ahead for a reservation to a top restaurant. The good news is–it's worth it.

Shut the Back Door! Just so you know, I'm exaggerating about this bread thing: One reviewer complained about not getting bread at Bâtard, saying that "How much would it cost you to offer regular baguettes cut in pieces?"

Other food terms to know:

- Sloppy Joe: a triple decker deli sandwich dressed with coleslaw and Russian dressing on thin-sliced rye bread–to die for.
- Beefsteak: a type of banquet where the host slices up tenderloin, usually for a fund-raising benefit.
- Sausage and Peppers: Italian style link sausage, bell peppers, and onions served in a sub roll.
- Philly Cheese Steak: Cheese Whiz and thin sliced steak. How can this be bad? It can't.
- Scrapple: a breakfast meat made from those parts of the pig that didn't make the sausage team. Those pieces are then mixed with corn meal and baked into a loaf. It's better than I make it sound—I'm surprised Southerners didn't think of it first.

The New York Survival Guide

- Polenta: ground corn, like grits but finer and from yellow or white corn.
- Taylor Ham: round Spam. Usually with egg and cheese on a roll.
- Gravy: slow cooked tomato sauce made with pork or beef.
- Marinara: quick tomato, sauce lighter in flavor than gravy.
- Baked Ziti: tube pasta baked with marinara.

Diners are the metro area's answer to Tim Horton or Shoney's. If there is a corner missing a pizza joint, chances are it has a diner on it. Diners sport laminated menus, fried foods, and display-cases containing fossilized deserts. You can order anything, anytime.

Pizza is good most anywhere in the metro area. Lombardi's in NYC or Stogie Joe's in Philadelphia often get the highest reviews. Of course, there are a lot of opinions on who's got the best—believe me you wouldn't be able to live on the difference between any of them. It's bread with cheese and tomato sauce. But, New Yorkers go on and on about pizza—just as I have.

Know the sacred words for Pizza:

- A slice—is just a plain cheese slice of pizza.
- A plain slice—is also a slice.
- Pie—refers to a whole pizza.
- Rays—is the generic term for pizza.
- Calzone - is pizza in folded form, like a giant turnover.
- Stromboli- rectangular folded. Or is it the Calzone? I forget which is which—and it really doesn't matter.

In a mystery that only New Yorkers care about, but I will reveal because it involves (what else?) pizza. Which of the ubiquitous Rays pizza joints below is the original and only one to visit?

The New York Survival Guide

- Famous Ray's
- World Famous Ray's
- Original Ray's
- Famous Original Ray's
- Ray Bari's
- Real Ray's
- One and Only Famous Ray's

*It's a trick question; the simply named "Ray's Pizza" closed in 2011. *When asked about the secret to making good pizza, the owner of Ray's Pizza said, "What do you mean? You buy top-grade flour. You buy very good mozzarella. What else?"*

If I didn't mention it, enjoy the bread, there is going to be a lot of it. Bread is good, staff of life and all that. How about "Man does not live by bread alone?" Here in Gotham you might.

This begs the question: Why is the bread better in New York? The New York metro area gets its water from rust belt tributaries that collect in open reservoirs. Polluted water works wonders for bakers and brewers. The water may not be safe to swim in, but okay to make bread.

Not for Nuttin'! *There is no need to be squeamish about E. coli as an ingredient. It dies at 180 degrees F. Bread bakes at 200 degrees F and pasta just north of that. E-coli cannot survive the alcohol in beer. Like in other 3rd world nations, you should drink beer, not water.*

Note to bakers, here's the list of common pollutants in the local water so that you might replicate the recipe: trichloroacetic acid, bromodichloromethane, chloroform, copper, dibromoacetic acid, dibromochloromethane, dichloroacetic acid, lead, monobromoacetic acid, monochloroacetic acid, total haloacetic acids (HAAs), total trihalomethanes (TTHMs) PCBs, and e-coli. Enjoy!

These pollutants make for great bread because carbon dioxide bubbles from the yeast readily attach themselves to the suspended particles. This makes the bread lighter as the pollutant particles enable the formation of larger and more numerous bubbles in the dough. (I'm completely making this part up—so go kill yourself.)

Fuhgeddaboudit! I suppose since there isn't much in the way of menu variety, diners entertain themselves by having sport with the wait staff. As you'll find out, the locals have lots of opinions. Here are a couple of bizarre exchanges:

- Customer: "Is your pasta made with eggs? I'm allergic to eggs."
- Owner: "No, there are not eggs in our pasta."
- Customer: "How can you be so sure?"
- Owner: "Because I made the pasta myself without eggs."
- Customer: "Nobody else would have thrown some eggs in it?"
- Owner: "Oh yes, now I remember. A vegan got loose in our kitchen and threw eggs all over. He may have thrown some in the pasta."
- Customer:" Really?"
- Owner:" No, not really. Now get the Hell out."
- Customer: "Really?"
- Owner: "Yes, Really."

And this charming episode:

- *Customer*: Unwrapping a piece of raw fish, "I want this salmon on my pizza."
- *Waiter*: "Uh, I can't do that."
- *Customer*: "Why not?"
- *Waiter*: "Well, first off this is a pizza place, not a sushi bar." And "..."
- *Customer*: Interrupting," I do it all the time. Make sure the cheese is melted, but the fish is cold. This is Maguro tuna you know."
- *Waiter*: "And, secondly, I'm sure it breaks about a dozen health codes. It's probably a crime of nature as well."
- *Customer*: "I want to see the manager."
- *Waiter*: "He's unavailable. We cut him up for fish bait the last time asked us to put sushi on a pizza.

Go Figure! Both stories involve dough; who could have guessed? New Yorkers know best. Deal with it.

The Classic Restaurants of New York

The restaurant scene changes overnight, but these establishments will probably continue to stand the test of time:

- The Palm, 837 2nd Ave, NYC, opened: 1926. The Palm has maintained a tradition of serving quality steaks and seafood. Though The Palm has expanded with restaurants across the U.S., this Palm is the first, and the walls are covered caricatures of celebrities, frequent guests, and favorite cartoon characters from the "Mad Men" era. The restaurant's motto is: "The place to see and be seen."
- Delmonico's, 56 Beaver St, NYC, opened: 1837. Delmonico's quickly established itself as one of the finest restaurants of New York City. Over the years, the restaurant has been patronized by Theodore Roosevelt, Mark Twain, and Napoleon III.

The New York Survival Guide

- Grand Central Oyster Bar, 89 E 42nd St, NYC, opened: 1913. The Grand Central Oyster Bar is a central feature of Grand Central Station and serves fine seafood from around.
- Keen's Steakhouse, 72 West 36 St, NYC, Opened: 1885. This Herald Square steakhouse became famous for its "Pipe Tradition." The membership of the Pipe Club has included Teddy Roosevelt, Babe Ruth, Will Rogers, Billy Rose, Grace Moore, Albert Einstein, George M. Cohan, J.P. Morgan, Stanford White, John Barrymore, David Belasco, Adlai Stevenson, General Douglas MacArthur, and "Buffalo Bill" Cody. Keen is known for its' excellent Mutton Chops.
- Peter Luger, 178 Broadway, NYC, opened: 1887. Peter Luger's has been ranked as the number one steak house in NYC for a generation. Though it can take months to get a dinner reservation, it's easy to get a table during the day. Be prepared for surly waiters! If you try a substitution—they might put a cap in your ass.
- PJ Clarke's, 915 3rd Ave, NYC, opened: 1884. P.J Clarke's serves some of the best pub grub and burgers in NYC. Expect the restaurant to be crowded at weekday happy hour.
- Kat'z Delicatessen, 205 E Houston St, NYC, opened: 1888. Katz's Deli serves some of the best Jewish-style deli sandwiches in NYC. The restaurant was featured in "When Harry Met Sally" and many other films. Katz's Deli is open late and so is a popular spot for late night munchies.
- Ralph's Italian Restaurant, 760 S 9th St, Philadelphia, opened: 1900. Terrific old school Italian. The place is always crowded and noisy. Enormous portions of……wait for it……….things made from wheat dough.
- McGillin's Olde Ale House, 1310 Drury Street, Philadelphia, opened: 1860. Good pub food and a great selection of local and regional beers on tap. McGillin's was named as "Best Irish Pubs in America" by *Complex* magazine & "Coolest bars in the U.S." by *Gourmet*.

Not for Nuttin'! By all means get a Zagat guide (it's pronounced "Zuh-Got") and leave it on your coffee table.

Don't Get Yourself Killed! New York City, alone, has about 30,000 restaurants. Trying them all would take about 28 years of eating out every meal. What to do? Find a restaurant you like and become a regular. You'll get a better table, goodies from the chef, and the wait staff will alert you if another diner is scheduled to be knocked off that evening.

Greeting the Natives

Greetings customs are in the extremes. They are the phatic expression, and the offer for 'sexual favors.

The greeting "howyadoin" isn't a question for you to answer. It's like saying "hey" to someone across the street. And like "hey," the proper response is to throw the term back at the person. They would be taken aback if you actually responded with something like, "I'm feeling better, but my mother is feeling poorly." To your audience an answer is a non sequitur.

In linguistics, the phrase "Howyadoin" is called a phatic expression, whose function is to perform a social task, as opposed to seeking information. The phrase "How are you doing" has lost its literal meaning in this context. Think of the phrase as less of a greeting and more a command to "speak!"

New Yorkers aren't the only culture who use phatic expressions. Here are examples from other countries:

- Botswana: "How did you wake?"
- Bhutan: "Is your body well?"
- Georgia: "Let you win."
- Iceland: "Happy"
- Mauritania: "On you no evil"
- Mauritius: "Speak!"
- Micronesia: "It was good."
- Moldova: "I kiss your hand."
- Niue: "Love be with you."
- Swaziland: "I see you!"
- Chinese: "Have you eaten?"

Other common greetings in New York:

- "Have you shaken someone down today?"
- "Just keep walking."
- "Hands up!"
- "Yo"
- "Nice ass"

The New York Survival Guide

On the other end of phatic greetings is the local practice of catcalling, also called "hollers." There is no way to avoid it. It is to the point where New York City is considering the establishment of "no catcall" zones.

Although construction workers and cabbies have the worst reputations, it is usually best to avoid eye contact with anyone, I repeat ANYONE on the street. Also, scowl fiercely. If inadvertent eye contact is made, look down or away. If verbal communication is attempted, feign hearing loss.

I've found that the forestry service "Bear Protocol" is perfect for fending off catcallers: <u>What to do if You See a Bear</u>, U.S. Department of the Interior. Here I just substituted "catcaller" for "bear," you'll notice it works incredibly well.

The New York Survival Guide

You may not see a catcaller during your visit because catcallers naturally avoid people. If you do see a catcaller, what you should do depends on the situation. In any case, always let a ranger know or leave a message at 911.

If you are in a developed area (e.g., campground, parking lot, lodging area) or if a catcaller approaches you, act immediately to scare it away: make as much noise as possible by yelling very loudly (don't worry about waking people up if it's nighttime.) If you are with other people, stand together to present a more intimidating figure, but do not surround the catcaller.

The intent is not to harm the bear, I mean catcaller, but to scare it from the area and restore its natural fear of people by providing a negative experience.

If you see a catcaller anywhere else, keep your distance (at least 50 yards, or about the distance four shuttle buses parked end to end would take up). If you get closer, you will be helping the catcaller become used to being around people. Catcallers that become comfortable around people lose their natural fear of us and sometimes become too aggressive; sometimes they then have to be killed.

When a ranger sees a catcaller, the ranger may use non-lethal aversive tactics to chase the catcaller out of a developed area. During your overnight stay, expect to see and hear rangers patrolling public areas for catcallers. You may hear rangers yelling at and chasing a catcaller. You may also see or hear rangers shooting noisemakers or non-lethal projectiles (such as rubber slugs from a shotgun or clear paintballs from a paintball gun). The intent is not to harm the catcaller but to scare it from the area and restore its natural fear of people by providing a negative experience.

Go Figure! *Pepper spray is illegal in both Yosemite and Philadelphia, but legal in NYC.*

Not for Nuttin'! *Since Philadelphia is the perennial winner of the "most unattractive people" award by* Travel and Leisure, *there would be no need for pepper spray anyhow.*

Catcall comebacks

The Forestry Service has good advice on dealing with man and beast, as I'm sure you'll agree. But what if a paintball toting Ranger isn't available? Best thing to do it ignore the catcallers. However, if you're feeling your oats here are some great comebacks:

Pretend you didn't hear the catcall and ask them to repeat it—the more they have to repeat the sillier they sound.

Hold eye contact, then slowly and deliberately stick your finger into your nose and dig for a winner.

Make mad-dog barking noises with eyes wide and full of crazy.

"I can't get angry at you today. It's Be Kind to Animals Week."

"Didn't I dissect you in biology class?"

Catcall: "Smile baby." Comeback: "I'll try smiling, if you try being smarter."

Catcall: "Hey baby." Comeback: "Call me baby again and I'll call you an ambulance."

Catcall: "Hey baby, what's your sign?" Comeback: "Do-not-bother."

Catcall: "Hey, how do you want your eggs in the morning?" Comeback: Unfertilized.

As a last resort, it's handy to keep a supply of Jets, 76ers, or Mets tickets in your purse. The tickets are cheap as these teams have sucked it up for years. If the bear...er.... I mean catcaller gets too close, throw the tickets up in the air and yell "Jets-Jets-Jets!"

Go Figure! *Mexico City catcalling led to female-only buses and subway cars. NYC is chock full of chivalry in comparison.*

Go Kill Yourself! Check out CNN's, "What 10 hours of street harassment in NYC looks like." What constitutes "harassment" is frequently that these denizens of depression in don't wish to communicate.

Don't Get Yourself Killed! In non-threatening situations, the greeting "howyadoin" is a greeting that serves as both a question and answer. Don't make eye contact or smile, as it may be considered a sign of weakness. Ladies: avoid construction sites, sporting events, or NYC during Restaurant Week.

Drink Until You Drop

These folks up here are serious about drinking. It's about getting hammered; it's not a social activity. The fact is that the closer to the poles, the more folks tend to drink. This is true all over the planet.

Southerners and Brits know how to drink. At one time most Americans did too. Several of our founding fathers made liquor. Ben Franklin enjoyed a pint or two, (well several pints— just look at him!) he also said, *"In wine there is wisdom, in beer there is freedom, in water there is bacteria."* By the way, you should never-ever drink water in Ben's hometown of Philadelphia. There is more than just bacteria in it now.

Befriending a Bartender Fast

You're going to need a good bartender for everything you learn about in this guide. They deserve to be treated well. Here is your guide to temporary happiness.

Getting their attention.

Be patient. There's no line to get drinks in your refrigerator for a good reason. Do not whistle, snap your fingers, or wave money: this should get you thrown out of the bar. If you're an expat, I don't need to tell you this. In my experience, the best way to approach a bartender is like you would a thoroughbred: calmly, don't yell or gesticulate. Maybe a sugar cube. Look the bartender square in the eye and say something like, "Hi, I can see you're very busy. When you get a chance could I order a drink, please? I'll be standing down there." Don't ever say, "I'll take care of you." –unless you are close enough to stroke the horse's nose.

Ordering drinks:

When the bartender comes over, have your order ready. Never ask for a "good pour." That's asking for a free drink and bartenders can get fired for that. If you're with a group, find out what each of them is drinking before you try to get the bartender's attention. Then put the drinks into logical order: cocktails, wine, and then beer.

Be aware that ordering a drink like a martini can open up a time-consuming question and answer routine. Know how you want it: "A dry Sapphire martini, Noilly Prat, straight up, olive." You're leaving the bartender no doubt that they are dealing with another professional,

If you want to run a tab, have a credit card ready by the time the bartender has poured your drinks. Even if you plan on paying with cash, chances are that the bartender will need a credit card for security. You might advise that you intend to pay with cash. You've let the bartender know they're dealing with a professional again—they love you already.

The New York Survival Guide

Tipping:

For the first drink, tip up to the cost of the drink in cash. Never tip a bartender on a free round. Thank him or her and tip big on the next round or when you close out. At the close of your tab, leave at least 20%.

Interacting with other patrons:

People go to bars for various reasons, not just to escape the din of the city, but also to have a nice conversation. Listen for the Locust Valley Lockjaw. Failing that, you should have been boning up on your ESPN coverage of pro sports. If you want to send a drink to someone you don't know, ask the bartender if it's a good idea. Never take off your suit jacket—you always look more sober with it on.

Other good advice for making a friend behind the bar

1. Don't argue with a bartender. They are always right.
2. If you only want one drink, go to communion.
3. Be a regular at more than one bar.
4. Always tip a little more than you should—it's a good investment.
5. Don't treat a bartender like they're waiting to find a real job.
6. Don't try ordering a drink from a bar-back.
7. Have a "go-to" drink in your repertoire, something simple. Whisky, beer, or wine. Take a sip, relax, and then figure out what you want to get hammered on.
8. When you're out with a group, put your damned phone away—using your phone is the yawn of the 21st century.

To Die For! Some bartenders will still use the "old school" signal of leaving an upside-down shot glass in front of you at the bar, especially if you are engaged in conversation or if the place is very noisy. It's no longer common, but if you find a bar that does this—it's the real deal. When you're ready for your drink, turn shot glass over. Even though the drink is free, the labor isn't. Don't forget to tip on the "buyback."

Don't Get Yourself Killed! Tip big and upfront at bars, restaurants, hotels, and casinos. It will more often than not improve the server's performance. Tipping after the service is over cannot improve your experience. Barista is not a real occupation. Bartender is. I've been saved more than once by the "cavalry of the countertop," and it's way cheaper than a psychiatrist's couch. More fun too. I've never met any girls in a shrink's office. Be polite and smile—hard currency most locals don't know about.

NYC Metro Liquor Laws

Here's a rundown of the liquor laws from the quad-state area; from simple easy to nightmare—make sure this book is downloaded on your mobile device.

Connecticut is the only state in the northeast that hasn't yet abolished Colonial era Blue Laws prohibiting the sale of alcoholic beverages on Sundays. Oddly enough, druggists in Connecticut must buy a liquor license even though they can't sell it.

New York liquor laws limit the sale of wine and spirits to liquor stores, but beer is available in convenience stores, delis, and grocery stores. Restaurants are technically prohibited from allowing patrons to BYOB, so that virtually all restaurants serve alcohol. Bars are closed four hours each day from 4 a.m. to 8 a.m.

New Jersey's drinking problem is that most restaurants don't have a liquor license. The number of licenses for each town is limited by the population of that town. Beer, wine, and liquor are all sold together. This means that most grocery stores cannot sell wine, beer, or liquor. This hasn't stopped New Jersey from achieving the 8th spot for both binge and underage drinking.

Pennsylvania is a bureaucrat's wet dream. Here's what you need to know.

Closing time for restaurants and bars in Pennsylvania is 2 a.m. and for private clubs is 3 a.m.

Wine and liquor are only sold in state-owned liquor stores, which don't sell beer. Hours are Monday through Saturday as early as 9 a.m., and they close as late as 10 p.m., subject to local laws. On Sunday, liquor may be sold from 12 p.m. until 5 p.m.

Wait, there's more...

In **Pennsylvania**, if you want a beer, how much you want to buy determines where you need to buy it. If you'd like a six pack, you'll have to find a restaurant with a Liquor Control Board license willing to sell beer over the counter. If you want to buy beer by the case or keg, you'll need to find one of the (usually well-hidden) **Pennsylvania-licensed** beer distributors. Beer distributors may sell by the case or keg only—no six packs or singles. The hours are similar to liquor stores. Although state law permits late-night beer sales, local authorities usually place additional restrictions so that stores typically close before 10 p.m. A special license is required to sell beer on Sundays (so not all do), and sales before 11 a.m. are not permitted.

Shut the Back Door! *You haven't lived until you've heard a drunken grandmother shouting "fuck you ref!" at MetLife Stadium*

Ya' Hump! *Nutcracker (def): homemade alcoholic beverage typically sold on trains or in parks out of a cooler.*

Shut the Back Door! *If you're stuck in Philly, bring a case of beer to your room. Drink it. Then go out. The whole place needs beer goggles.*

Masterclass Drinking in NYC

General George Patton would drink a shot of vegetable oil before a big night. Another method worked out by a chemist and Sam Adams founder Jim Koch enables him to stay sober, all night long.

Take a package of yeast, mix it in with yogurt, and eat one teaspoon per beer right before you start drinking.

Apparently, this works because dry yeast has an enzyme in it called alcohol dehydrogenases (ADH) that is able to break alcohol molecules down into their constituent parts of carbon, hydrogen, and oxygen. This is the same thing that happens when your body metabolizes alcohol in its liver. The trick is to have that enzyme in your stomach when the alcohol first hits it so that the ADH will begin breaking it down before it gets into your bloodstream and, thus, your brain. It will mitigate—not eliminate—the effects of alcohol.

Hangover Cures for Pros

What if the yeast and yogurt trick doesn't work? Here are the classic hangover cures.

- Grapefruit juice and Juicy Fruit gum.
- A Mountain Dew and a Mr. Goodbar.
- Underberg Bitters or Angostura bitters, some soda and a dash of lemon.
- Mix 1 egg yolk, 1 tsp. powdered sugar, 2 oz. brandy, cayenne pepper.
- Big fatty breakfast, a 5-mile run, sex. Not all at once.
- A big, greasy cheeseburger accompanied by a chocolate milkshake.
- Shakes on a Plane: 1 ounce Angostura bitters, 3/4 ounce Falernum liqueur.
- Prolong the agony with a Bloody Mary.
- Pabst Blue Ribbon Beer, orange juice, raw egg.
- Two Goody's shaken up in a quart of Gatorade or coconut water.
- Eat cracklings the night of a big drink.

Everyone swears by a hangover cure—even though we all know it's illusory. Except...the last on this list, cracklings. And that's not my opinion, it's the conclusion of the *British Medical Journal*. The Brits, useful lads, discovered the cure for hangovers: bacon and bread.

It turns out that the bacon is a "super food." Alcohol depletes the neurotransmitters that enable your body to process information like determining the attractiveness of the blond at the bar or charm of Philadelphia. The carbohydrates of the bread and the protein in bacon breaks down into amino acids, which replenishes the neurotransmitters that alcohol depleted.

Don't Get Yourself Killed! Don't drink and drive. Although the culture of acceptance has changed, too many people try to drive home. The yeast and yogurt trick won't work. Take an Uber or taxi—they are those yellow vehicles trying to hit you at crosswalks.

Conversation in New York

"A conversation is a dialogue, not a monologue. That's why there are so few good conversations, due to scarcity, two intelligent talkers seldom meet." Truman Capote.

Conversation is a considered an art form in the American South and West Africa. In the New York metro area, it's an opportunity for conquest. You might be used to the give and take similar to tennis: One person speaks, the other listens. Repeat.

Conversation in NYC = People with Fire Hoses.

At first this noisy battle may seem as pointless as a "monkey humping a football"; however, the combatants are not exchanging information. It's a duel to the death—or maybe to the deaf. The duel is probably a pizza controversy and or some other pointless dustup regarding the Mets, Phillies, or Nets.

Not for Nuttin'! *Beware of the "elevator ambush," where escape from Mets, Phillies, and Nets chitchat is impossible.*

Go Figure! *How to know who has won? Whoever stops talking first has surrendered.*

NYC Conversation Starters

How to engage a local? Remember since everything sucks, effective communication should begin with a complaint. Don't say: "Hello, isn't it a lovely day?" Say: "Yo, last week's weather sucked!" Complaining has a social function: it gives us a sense of togetherness in adversity. Want to start a conversation with a New Yorker? Here are their favorite complaints:

1. The stench of summer in the City.
2. The insanely high rent.
3. Time Warner Cable.
4. Tourists.
5. The Bridge and Tunnel people.
6. The L train and the G train.
7. Walking through Times Square.
8. Cash-only restaurants.
9. Long lines at Shake Shack.
10. Subway pole-leaners.
11. Oversized umbrellas.
12. Boston.

The New York Survival Guide

What constitutes rudeness varies from culture to culture. For example, thumbs-up in Italy, Greece, and the Middle East is basically telling a local: "up yours!" In Japan and Korea, you'll likely offend wait staff if you leave a tip. Don't eat with your left hand around Arabs. And if you get in the backseat of a taxi in Australia, the driver will think you're a wanker.

The difficulty in the New York metro is that a third of New Yorkers were not born in the United States. The largest groups are from the Dominican Republic, China, Jamaica, Guyana, Mexico, Ecuador, Haiti, Trinidad and Tobago, Colombia, and Russia.

So, it's not because New Yorkers hate you or want to hurt you (just yet anyhow), it's that they just don't know what custom is required. Because keeping up with all this diversity is impossible, locals have their own code of conduct, or what I like to call "The Pseudo Guido."

Speaking like a local is less about what you say, and more about how you gesticulate. Wild gestations are required for authenticity. New Yorkers are known for being direct, opinionated, and unflinchingly confident—for no apparent reason.

NYC Terms and Vocabulary List

- Agita: nerves from worry or stress. As in "you kids are giving me agita.":
- Allriteallready: I'm going to do it, stop nagging.
- Atomic bomb—the largest and ugliest woman in a group.
- Axe: "ask"
- Blind Eels: yet another name for condoms washing up on the beach.
- Bo-nasty: someone who is dressed skanky.
- Boss: what counter service calls you instead of "sir." FTI, "Pal", "Buddy", or "Chief" means you are in deep manure.
- Braciole: a euphemism for male genitalia.
- Break the Devil's Dishes: to fly in the face of reason.
- Butana: a skank.
- Carfare: a subway token.
- Chess: a body part.
- Chest: the game of Chess.

The New York Survival Guide

- Chips: you break it, you bought it. Example: "If you break that glass, chips."
- Coney Island Whitefish: condoms that wash up on the beach at Coney Island.
- Corner Man: a lookout.
- Cugine: (Coo JEEN) a "guido."
- Cugutza: a hard-headed person.
- Cujinette: a guidette.
- Dees. Doze. Dat: These. Those. That.
- Dollars to Doughnuts: a sure thing.
- Downtown: To say you're going downtown means that you're going to in the Street area. The whole of Manhattan is referred to as "the City."
- Duh-ta-duh: an idiot or oaf.
- Dutch: a do-over.
- Earl: oil
- Egg Creme: a drink made of club soda, milk, and syrup.
- El: subway tracks that run on a trestle over the street.
- Ferclempt: heart in your throat, emotional.
- Filgia de butana: daughter of a skank.
- Fins (Or Finsies): a game of "not it," saying mean the same thing.
- For all intensive purposes: contraction of the phrase "For all intents and purposes."
- Fugazy: not on the up and up.
- Fuggedaboudit: never mind.
- Gates Are Closed: no one else can be admitted or join the game.
- Gavoon: a knucklehead, also spelled Gavone.
- Give him leather: kick someone who is down.
- Go kill yourself: get lost.
- Go See Where You Gotta Go: stop wasting my time.
- Goof: a good time, as in "oh, we had a goof" or to kid someone.
- Goombah: good ole' boy.
- Grow Legs: something that's likely to be stolen.
- Guy shopping: finding a man.
- He don't know from nothin': he's not very bright.

The New York Survival Guide

- Hero: a po'boy sandwich, also: grinder, sub or hoagie.
- Hey Haya-dooin: a greeting.
- Hindoo: a do-over during a game.
- Hiya: a greeting.
- Hook you up: to give to someone a good deal or take care of them.
- Hoowah: a prostitute.
- Indian: an extremely tanned Caucasian.
- Jacked hideous: incredibly unattractive.
- Jeet?: did you eat?
- Jeet-jet?: did you eat yet?
- Jersey Turnpike: a dance move in which a woman jams her rear end against a man's crotch and then bends over.
- Jimmies: chocolate sprinkles for ice cream.
- Johnny Pump: fire hydrant.
- Keep Chicky: to keep a lookout.
- Lemmegetta: let me get a, as in, "Lemmegetta tuna on rye", or "Lemmegetta most expensive thing on your menu."
- Marone: a mild swear word, to be used when someone jumps the line.
- Manzo le gausha: "Between your legs!" a mild curse.
- Meatball: a woman who is short and well fleshed out.
- Mung-go: any scrap that can be salvaged and sold.
- Neutral: to begin anew.
- Not for Nuttin': a phrase often used before telling someone the truth.
- Off the hook: out of control.
- Only in New York!: what is said when you walk by the homeless man letting his balls hang out.
- Pino: Pinot Grigio wine
- Polly Noses: The helicopter-like maple seed cases.
- Potsy: hopscotch.
- Putting Chinese on the Ball: to "jinx" the ball during a game.
- Putz: a Yiddish insult that's often used by people who don't know it means "penis."

The New York Survival Guide

- Right here!: a threat uttered while pointing to one's crotch.
- Ruff: "roof."
- Scash: an old car beat up car.
- Schmeboygah: a slob.
- Scootch (Or Scutch): someone who is a pain in the ass.
- Scumbag: a dishonest jerk.
- She Thinks Who She Is: someone who has a high opinion of themselves.
- Shem: a jerk or a stupid person.
- Shlub: a slob or clumsy oaf.
- Shongod: someone who's all messed up, slovenly, or a bum.
- Skank Ho: yet another word for a woman of questionable morals.
- Skeeved out: repulsive.
- Skel: a lowlife person.
- Skinny Molink: someone who is sickly thin.
- Skitching: skating by hanging onto a vehicle on icy streets, also done with a skateboard.
- Skive: a cheat.
- Sliding Pond: a playground slide.
- Slop Tart: a woman who is drunk and sloppy.
- Sloppopotamus: a large Slop Tart
- Stick Ball: street baseball played with a broom handle and a "Spaldeen."
- Stick pins in my eyes: very frustrated.
- Stood: the past tense of "stay." As in "I knew I shoulda stood in bed."
- Stoop: the front stairs of your building, often where people hang out.
- Tar Beach: the roof of an apartment building when used in the summer for sunbathing.
- The Bomb: the best, as in "the new Yankee Stadium is the bomb."
- Tree: the number three. Also, a term of endearment for a tall person.
- True: through. as in "you gotta go true the tunnel to get to Jersey."
- Wack/Whack: depending on circumstances, it could mean crazy or killed.
- Walking holiday: someone who is always having a good time.

The New York Survival Guide

- Wallear: to have an uncontrollable desire for something.
- Weasel Deal: a dishonest deal.
- Weisenheimer: a smart ass.
- What: barking the word "what" is the accepted answer to almost all inquiries.
- Whats-amatta-feru: What's the problem?
- Whiz Wit: a cheesesteak sub with onions. (Whiz is "Cheese-Whiz.")
- Who died and made you boss?: phrase used for letting someone know they're not running the show.
- Yooze, Youse guys: instead of "y'all". The plural of "you."
- You Got a Lotta Shit Wichoo: you have some nerve.
- Your Mother's Ass: an all-purpose curse.
- Your Sister's Got a Head: a mild curse.

The New York Survival Guide

One comment from a reviewer said, "It's insulting to think that everyone from New York speaks that way. People from Brooklyn speak differently than people from Long Island, who speak differently than people from The Bronx and certainly Philly—they are a bunch of knuckle draggers. This list of phrases is awful and stereotypical!"

To this, I say: "Get outta heeer! Whadda ya tawkin' aboud? You gonna let deez muthafuckas change yuz? Fuhgeddaboutit! Yuz tell dem come hea-ah n' den, yuz sez to dem: get da fuck outta heyah!"

Not for Nuttin! Men, prepare to have "y" tacked to the end of your name. It seems that everyone needs an "Italian-ized" name. Vincent is Vinny. Paul is Pauli. Guido is—ah well, Italian enough I suppose.

Don't get yourself killed! The locals aren't interested in pleasantries. If it's a beautiful day, keep it to yourself. Remember that complaints lead to conversation, or at least a gesticulation contest. You can't go wrong complaining about Boston. Speak in an "outside voice" at all times, and, don't forget, you gotta usa yur hands!

The New York Survival Guide

The Great Outdoors.

Like golf? Tips to Get Tee-time

- Pull up to the course in a Bomb Squad Van.
- Walk around the property in IRS gear. The parking lot will clear out, guaranteed.
- Buy your tee time from a broker—no really!
- Take up miniature golf. Anybody can play on a big course. Try putting through a windmill.
- Call up and say, "We're traveling through your state and wanted to play a little golf and were wondering if we'd have any problem bringing a carload of weapons onto the golf course?
- Call up and ask for a tee time between 12:00 and noon. No one ever asks for that time.
- It's a well-kept secret that the 10 p.m. tee time is kept open.

- Wear your green Masters jacket.
- Bring Phil Mickelson with you.
- Rip a hole through the time-space continuum by letting someone merge into your lane on your way to the club.

Camping, Hiking, and, Hunger Games

The New Jersey outdoor website doesn't have enough for me to make fun of. They suggest hiking in abandoned mines and camping in a parking lot. I never understood the attraction of camping in an urban area. Are you supposed to hang your beer from a tree so the locals don't paw through it?

New Jersey may be willing to cede the outdoors. But fortunately for me, you, and this guide, New York City came through with lots of things to poke fun at.

The New York Survival Guide

Bouldering in Central Park.

Picnickers and outdoor enthusiasts flock to Central Park, but this world-famous green space has also become the epicenter of New York's outdoor climbing community. Bouldering is a like rock climbing—only unchallenging. It doesn't require ropes, but you'll need a strong stomach to overcome homeless camps. Try Cat Rock, Wave Rock, and (I wish I was making this last name up) Rat Rock.

Nature walking in Inwood Hill Park.

This is the site of one of the best transactions in real estate history: Peter Minuit's purchase of Manhattan from the Lenape Indians for about $25 in beads. From the park, there is hardly any evidence of the desolation the beads bought.

Mountain biking in Wolfe's Pond Park: Staten Island is probably most famous for it's the ferry (something the deer apparently know about). You'll find a variety of terrain—glacial ponds, sandy beaches, and hidden bodies.

Canoeing on Gowanus Canal.

Paddle on one of the most polluted bodies of water in North America. It's a Superfund site that's clean enough to support growing numbers of crabs. The Gowanus Dredgers Canoe Club leads free tours of the canal from April to October.

Sailing lessons at Flushing Meadows Corona Park.

The 1,255-acre former dumping ground, Flushing Meadows offers more than a funny and punny potty name: the 1964 World's Fair, the New York Hall of Science, and the New York Field of Failure, (Citi Field, home of the Mets). Also, the American Small Craft Association offers lessons that will teach you basics of escaping the New York metro area by sea.

The New York Survival Guide

Bird Watching in Prospect Park.

An important Atlantic Flyway for North American birds, more than 200 species can be seen feet-up at the park depending on the season. On Saturdays at 12:30 p.m., the park's Audubon Center leads one-hour bird-watching tours for free. After your visit, grab a ride home with an armored car at nearby Grand Army Plaza.

Sleeping under the stars in New York.

The New York City parks department offers an innovative—and family-friendly—program that allows you to sleep outside on sidewalks, benches, and heating grates all over the city. The staff of Urban Park Rangers will lead you on a variety of activities, from cooking out to panhandling.

Paddling the Bronx River: The Bronx River is New York City's only "true" river and an environmental success story. Once strewn with refuse and bodies, these days it harbors escaped pet turtles, alligators, and pythons.

Trail Running in Van Cortlandt Park.

A nice escape from the tedium of pounding the payment in midtown. The cross-country course has become is a grueling test of endurance through dense woods and an undulating hills and dales. No joke, it's pretty good.

Skateboarding in TriBeCa.

The old piers of Manhattan's West Side are slowly being transformed into the city's newest parkland. The "street-style" venue has the extra feature of being constructed on century old planks, so that thrill of plunging into the Hudson is a bonus.

The thing I admire about Philadelphia is they don't even pretend, they just come out and tell you that the only outdoor activity is getting to Lincoln Financial Field (Eagles stadium). The following is from Philadelphia's Official Global Convention and Visitors Site:

"With nine professional sports teams, four state-of-the-art arenas, numerous annual events, including the Philadelphia Marathon and regattas, and a community that loves a good game, Philadelphia is the country's best city for taking in a sporting event. (i.e. No sporting life.)

City streets are tree-lined and surprisingly intimate, all leading to signature parks that define each neighborhood. Parks are safe, with activities part of the daily life of the people and families who come to relax, eat, play and stroll." (Oh, just never mind, the parks are safe.)

I recommend hiking through Eastern State Prison or exploring many of the other rust belt relics. A favorite attraction is the ruins of the Bethlehem Steel plant just north in Allentown, which also has a casino.

Note: Philadelphia, or "Filthy-delphia," has, for an uncountable number of years, ranked as the ugliest U.S. city by *Travel and Leisure*. Also, in an interesting twist that is just crying out for a taxpayer funded study, *Travel and Leisure* also ranked Philly dead last in the "attractive people" category out of 30 major American cities. Possibly because of this unwanted attention, Philadelphia also ranked as extremely unfriendly (26th out of 30) and not the least bit athletic

(28th out of 30) in the same year. You might be thinking I could make a lot more jokes about Philly's plight—but I don't believe in kicking someone when they're dead.

Urban Camo

Expats and visitors often misinterpret slovenly dressed locals as indifference, but it's actually a survival tactic—urban camouflage. Consulates and insurance companies both advise visitors to blend into the urban landscape because criminals typically pick their victims based on appearance. Don't let yourself stand out as an easy target. Get your black on—and stop smiling for God's sake!

Thieves know that visitors often carry enough money to get them through their sentence—sorry, I mean "stay." Plus, a thief has a better chance of taking down a newcomer than a local. Locals might be packing heat. Leave the Brooks Brothers, Lilly, and LL Bean at home, unless you find a gaggle of Locust Valley folks to hide amongst.

The other camouflage strategy that work well is logo apparel of a pro sports team. The fashion brands here are the Jets, Mets, and Devils. Or Giants, Yankees, and Rangers. Or Eagles, Phillies, and Flyers.

Not for Nuttin'! Warning: You may not mix and match. Wearing a Giants, Mets, Flyers ensemble would rip open the very fabric of the space-time continuum.

Shut the Back Door! Did I forget about the NBA? Nope. There hasn't been a professional level basketball team in the area since 1983 when the Philadelphia 76'ers won the NBA championship. If you wear NBA gear, the locals will think you're from LA.

Next question you need to be prepared for is: what name do you put on your new jersey? I'm thinking, (and I hope you are) why, my name of course! Wrong answer. You show your love for highly paid professional athletes by wearing that man's name on your back. It's just like in high school when girls wore their boyfriend's letterman jacket with their name on it—the difference is that it's without benefits—I think.

Not for Nuttin! If you're still convinced you need another man's name on your clothing, consider the economics when players switch teams. Are you still going to wear your LeBron James Heat jersey? Too bad you burned your LeBron Cavalier jersey now that he's ~~back at the Cavaliers~~ with the Lakers.

Go Kill Yourself! The record for pro players changing teams is 13 in MLB, 12 in the NFL, 11 in the NBA, and 8 in the NHL. That's a lot of laundry.

Go Figure! Giants' fans are considered classy by the standards of the northeast, at least when compared to Jet's and Eagles fans.

Go Kill Yourself! Sweatshirts, gym shorts, running shoes, and exercise gear are always appropriate, especially if you look like you could chase down a would-be assailant.

Not for Nuttin! Nix the fanny pack, instead buy a backpack. Put a brick in it so that you can defend yourself.

Avoiding Burial Expenses

The key is to blend in and avoid standing out. There's really no upside to being identified as fresh meat. Like hyenas on the Serengeti, the locals can evaluate someone within seconds for their prey value. For many who travel, immersion into the local culture is the best part of the adventure, and it avoids burial expenses.

Pro Tips for Blending In

1. Don't stare: no matter what, pretend you have seen it all.
2. Make-up, hair, deodorant: remember that less is more.
3. Confidence is key. If a pigeon poops on your shoulder, it was all part of the plan.
4. Wrong footwear will give you away. Wear flats or converse high-tops.
5. Walk on the right side of the sidewalk at a brisk pace, even if you don't know where you're going.
6. Prepare in advance for the Metro Card turnstile by having the card ready to swipe.

The New York Survival Guide

7. Don't complain about high prices in stores, restaurants, parking, etc.
8. Don't look up at the buildings—unless you see a jumper, then egg them on. But first try to find out if they sublet.
9. New Yorkers fold their pizza. Seriously, this is always on a list.
10. If you spot a celebrity, ignore them.

Don't Get Yourself Killed! If you are hell bent on wearing pro sports gear, don't wear gear from teams outside the metro area. Especially provocative is any Boston team. Also, it's dangerous to wear Giants gear in Jersey, or Jets stuff in Long Island. Wear NHL gear only if you want to fight, people will figure as a hockey fan you like to.

Bottom line: It's easier and safer wearing black. Fit your mood to your clothing and no one will mess you. Don't forget to gesture!

Tipping

History of Tipping

Though tipping may seem like an America invention, the custom is borrowed from European aristocracy. The practice began sometime in the 16th century when guests at English estates were expected to give a small gratuity for good service. In this way, the aristocracy discovered a method of cutting overhead by simply making their guests pick up the tab. Soon, the custom spread to inn keepers, cab drivers, and baristas.

Prior to the Civil War, Americans did not tip. After the war, the newly rich, war-bucked yankees visited Europe and brought the tipping practice back home to show off their newfound gentility.

A *New York Times* article of the period stated that, "Once tipping got hold in the United States, it spread rapidly like evil insects and weeds." By the 1900s, Americans considered tipping to be the norm, and, in fact, were frequently criticized for over-tipping by Europeans. Englishmen complained that their servants felt shortchanged and that Americans received poorer service because they were not experienced in dealing the servant class.

Go Kill Yourself! The custom of tipping is an often overlooked consequence of the South losing the Civil War.

The word "tip" is believed to have been coined by the English writer, Samuel Johnson. Johnson frequented a coffee-shop which had a bowl labeled "To Insure Promptitude." Johnson and other guests would put a coin into the bowl throughout the evening to receive better service. Soon, the label was shortened to "T.I.P." and then to simply "tip".

Ya Hump! For my money TIP should stand for "Trick Innocent Patrons."

As tipping spread from the Northeast, many Americans found it to be incompatible with democracy and equality. In 1891, journalist Arthur Gaye wrote that a tip was to be given to someone "who is presumed to be inferior to the donor, not only in worldly wealth, but in social position also." In William Scott's book, *The Itching Palm*, he pointed out that tipping was tantamount to paying for a service twice: once to the employer, and once to the employee. "Tipping," he wrote, "is an aristocratic idea that Americans left Europe to escape."

A handful of states had anti-tipping laws, but by 1926 they had been repealed.

Tipping again changed in the 1960s when Congress agreed that workers could receive a lower minimum wage if a portion of their salary came from tips. Observers have noted that because waiters live off their tips, tipping in the United States is more mandatory than voluntary, and so good service is coincidental.

Shut the Back Door! Research on tipping suggests the pleasure derived from giving change to inferiors may be why we continue to tip today.

Go Figure! Until very recently, most travelers didn't tip hotel maids. Marriott changed all that with an initiative that helped establish the practice as standard. Today about 70% of Americans tip maids, as recently as 2011 it was 30%.

Not for Nuttin! Where you leave the money matters. Marriott provides envelopes for housekeeping gratuities. Otherwise, the maid may not know who the money is for. In one online forum, a maid advised that hotel guests should leave the tip where it's obviously for the cleaning staff (bathroom) and not for the call girl (bedside).

According to a PayScale study, the median restaurant tip is now 19.5%. Many restaurants are suggesting that 25% to 30% is the proper gratuity level, and that a 20% tip, once considered generous, is the minimum. As recently as 2008 an *f* tipping guide stated "15% for good service is still the norm" at American restaurants. An American Demographics study from 2001 found that three-quarters of Americans tipped an average of 17% on restaurant bills.

So how do you know what tip to leave? Watch for cues from the wait staff. Is your waitress attractive? Attractive waitress who wear make-up, brush lightly against you, and have ornamentation in their hair expect generous tips. If the wait staff repeats your order, introduces themselves, or pulls out photos of their kid's prep school advisor, they expect a big tip.

Go Figure! Studies show that the quality of service has very little effect on how much you should tip.

Go Kill Yourself! The tip your wait staff expects depends on your age and ethnicity. If you are a Millennial, Hispanic, or Black, you can leave 15% tips because that is what the wait staff expects. And if you're Italian, just skip tipping altogether, in a recent survey only 11% give gratuities.

The Madam of good manners, Emily Post, wrote: "You will not get good service unless you tip generously," and went on to say, "Tipping is undoubtedly a bad system, but it happens to be in force, and, that being the case, travelers have to pay their share of it—if they like the way made smooth and comfortable."

Not for Nuttin'! Sex workers are tipped more than any other group. Coincidentally, Dads tip babysitters, but moms do not. Just sayin'.

Clever Ways to Avoid Tipping

Here are several fun ways you can avoid paying a mandatory gratuity for poor service:

1. Request an 18% discount for a large party. Why would they do that? Because you have a large party and the restaurant will not want to miss the volume, that's why.

2. Break up your party into separate tables. Breaking up your party into several adjacent tables is another preemptive move that has the added benefit of ensuring you'll probably get better service. Kind of fun too. You can mix and match dinner partners each time the server leaves, so that the servers are sure to get the orders wrong, and you can justifiably tip less.

3. Negotiate with the manager after you're seated. Okay, enough for the preemptive suggestions. Let's assume you've already sat down with your large party. You're still holding all the cards. They won't want to lose you. Negotiate to have the mandatory tip taken off, and a discount.

4. Inform the manager you'd like a different server. If you're not getting good service, talk to the manager and request another server. Although it is doubtful the manager will comply with your request, the odds are they will help ensure the rest of your meal goes smoothly. Often times, a chat with the manager will result in some sort of compensation for your troubles such as complimentary appetizers or meals—which offsets a portion of the mandatory gratuity.

5. Last resort, dispute the tip with your credit card company. The restaurant manager was as useless as a cow on crutches. Your food was cold, and the drinks didn't have ice. Stay calm; revenge is at hand. Pay your bill and make sure you use a credit card. Send a polite letter to the restaurant detailing the poor service you received and requesting your tip money back. Then call your credit card company and threaten to cancel the card if they don't remove the gratuity. This works for the same reason that calling to cancel your cable provider gets you a better deal. Clever, huh?

Not for Nuttin'! Many restaurants in the area add 18% gratuity. I would not count on the goodwill of the wait staff to alert you in the case where you've added your tip on top of the mandatory gratuity.

If All Else False, How to Yank the Waiters Chain

- If negotiation doesn't work, or you just want to have some fun, make sure you get good value for your gratuity money!
- Ignore the check for an awkward time period, then split the bill between several cards and cash with all the diners.
- Switch seats every time the waiter leaves.
- Ask everybody to slip the waiter their (fake) number.
- Tip in change.
- Claim it is everyone's birthday at the table. One person at a time.
- Send a half-eaten entrée back: "Oh, I didn't like this. Can I get something else?"
- Leave new age, religious, and offbeat literature at each place setting.

- Use your phone to time the waiter where he will notice.
- Stack all the plates and glasses in a tower in the center of the table.
- Ask for dessert menus—don't order any. And coffee—lots of coffee.

Tip Amounts for All Services in NYC

Seems like everyone in their area has their hand out. I wonder why vending machines don't have tip cups? Probably because no one has thought if it. At any rate, here is the current suggested tips for services:

- Bellman/Porter: $5-10 per bag. More if there are bodies in them.
- Concierge: Tipping is why these people exist on earth. The more difficult the request, the higher the tip.
- Counter service/fast-food restaurants: If you make eye contact, tip a dollar and whatever change they hand you.
- Dealers at Casinos: 5% of winning or bet amount at end of session.
- Drink Servers: Start heavy $10 or more: remember "To Insure Promptitude." After that, $1-$2 per drink.
- Hairdresser/manicurist: 10% if they sound like Fran Drescher: 20%.
- Hotel housekeeping: 2-5% of the nightly rate, more if there are more than three people in a room. Leave the tip each day when you leave the room. If you have additional items delivered to your room, such as extra pillows, hangers, luggage racks, etc, tip the person who brings them $5.
- Hotel limo driver: For a "free" ride from the airport, $10 - $20.
- In-suite dining wait staff: You will be paying a service charge or convenience fee, which goes to the hotel and a separate 20% gratuity.
- Spa: For a massage—10%. Happy ending—50%. And leave a small gratuity for the spa attendant who showed you around the Spa: $2 to $5.
- Taxi Driver: 10-15% of fare, based near misses.
- Tour Guides: 15% - 20%, depending on quality and getting you out of the Bronx in one piece.

- Valet Parking Attendants: $2 - $5 depending on new dents.

FAQ Regarding Gratuities.

1. Am I legally required to tip anywhere in the U.S.? No. Service charge is always voluntary, even when it's added to your bill. But if you deduct gratuity from the check, don't expect it to go down well.

2. Why should I tip? Under federal law, the minimum wage for tipped employees like bartenders and waitresses is just $2.13 per hour. Shaking customers down for tips switches the burden of paying a living wage to you.

3. How much should I tip in restaurants? 15–25% See advice on whether they expect it, and how much. High-end restaurants will expect 25%. Don't forget the maitre d' and the homeless guy holding the door open for you.

4. Do I need to leave an extra tip if my bill says, "gratuity included"? No, although this usually happens only if you're a party of eight or more. Some tourist joints add a service charge, presumably because they know foreigners don't care, it's only American money.

5. Why do waiters always ask, "Do you need change?" This is Gotham for "stand and deliver." If you pay in cash, your server will almost always deliver this line as they snatch up your check. You might feel intimidated. Don't. In all likelihood your waiter is already working his next victim.

6. What should I tip in bars? Tip big on the first order, up to the price of the drink. Keep the tips flowing and you might get your fifth or sixth drink free. Bars with table service will expect at least a 10% tip at the end of the night.

7. What about tipping taxi drivers? If a driver helps with your bags and takes a good route, 20% is reasonable. Just joking. This ain't London. Not only will you be carrying your own bags, but you'll probably be helping the driver with his English pickup lines.

The New York Survival Guide

8. Do I have to tip when I queue up at a lunch or coffee kiosk? No. But the coffee in the New York metro is weaker than dishwater. What I suggest is putting the cost of the beverage in the tip jar and leaving the beverage there. Technically, buying over the counter is gratuity-free. If the person in front of you drops in a dollar, so what. Be strong damn you!

9. What's likely to happen if I don't tip? It depends. Is the person armed? Are they Italian, Puerto Rican, or Chinese? If so, leave a tip. Tip the English because Brits in the service industry are rarer than a diamond in a bobcat's ass. Irish? Nothing, they're used to be screwed by the Brits. Indian? Nothing, they are too damned polite to complain.

10. When shouldn't I tip? Anytime when you think you can safely get away with it.

Profile of the New Yorker

Everyone in NYC is subject to a classification: race, religion, and orientation. The goal of the locals is to figure out where you belong. This can take some doing. There are as many as 800 languages spoken in Gotham and 176 languages spoken by students of the NYC public schools.

Where you live determines who you are. This is why New Yorkers talk a lot about streets. One of the first things you're asked is, "Where do you live?" You might think, "This person wants to be friends and get together sometime." No. The locals do this to form an opinion on your beliefs and net worth.

The New York Survival Guide

Here's what all the neighborhoods mean

If you say:" 5th Avenue" or "Central Park West,"

> They hear: "I'm just back from Musha Cay, and I'm here because I felt like slumming. I have no taxable income. I serve on a dozen charity boards I give a shit about, and my trust fund is larger than the GDP of Costa Rica."

If you say: "Tribeca" or "The Financial District" (the alternative answer is "Goldman Sachs," a place of business—it says, exactly, the same thing.)

> They hear: "I'm on Wall Street and make more money in a day that you do in a year, and I just wanted you to know that fact. I know you want to be me."

If you say: Upper East Side,

> What they hear: I'm Jewish, an entertainment executive or personal injury lawyer. I make enough to cover the rent, but the apartment is my bank account. I'm single, and it looks like it's staying that way."

If you say: Upper West Side,

> They hear: "I'm a mid –level investment banker, and I'm cooler than the Upper East Side. I'm possibly gay. I made it on my own. I make enough to cover the rent and split a summer rental in the Hamptons with 20 people."

If you say: Any other areas of NYC south of Central Park and north of Canal.

They hear: "I'm trying to break into a banking or an entertainment job that will let me ditch my five roommates in our 4th floor walkup for a studio apartment. Meanwhile, I'm deceiving myself by writing a novel and auditioning for off-off Broadway. Sometimes I have enough money to splurge on Chinese."

If you say: "I'm looking for an apartment in any one of the previous areas,"

They hear: "I'm living in Harlem and earning enough for rent and ammunition. I'm hanging out here in the hopes a cougar takes me home."

If you say: "Staten Island," "Brooklyn," "Bronx," or "Queens,"

They hear: "I'm living on the same street with the rest of my family. I'm a doorman. Pizza. Jets. Mets.

If you say: "New Jersey," "Pennsylvania," or "Connecticut,"

They hear: "I've traded the dream for a 3-hour commute and haven't had sex in the last year. I'm hoping someone from Park Avenue adopts me."

The New York Survival Guide

Who Gets to Be a New Yorker?

New Yorkers have an opinion on who is actually a New Yorker. This from a Native New Yorker on who is and isn't a New Yorker, and I quote:

"If u did not attend school in NYC from grades 1 - 12 u are not a New Yorker if u moved here for college u live here u are not a New Yorker if u a are a super rich upper west side parents loft in Williamsburg u are not a New Yorker a New York has lived in the city mainly a outter boro New Yorkers are built from the struggle I'm sick of these upper class imports who built there ideas of a New York life off of friends plus they distance their selves from the " ghetto natives " f**k u , ur internship and ur sublease from daddy's old college buddy"

New Yorker Street Cred

So, a native New Yorker must be born and educated in the City, but not live in Williamsburg or the Upper West Side. Also, they can't have gotten an internship or a good deal on a sublease. Undoubtedly, there are opinions on what constitutes a New Yorker, but if you follow these guidelines you may pass for one:

- ✓ An inability or lack of desire to drive.
- ✓ Bark directions at cab drivers.
- ✓ Be desperate enough to have ridden in the empty train car. (It stinks.)
- ✓ Be free of patience for everything and everyone.
- ✓ Be suspicious towards everything and everyone.
- ✓ Believe that all parades are just a bad idea.
- ✓ Discomfort in nature: crickets, squirrels, sunshine, etc.
- ✓ Drink a 40oz malt liquor from a paper bag.
- ✓ Drink a quarter water. Those brightly colored drinks now cost $1.
- ✓ Genuine confusion over Australians: Isn't that the giant ice continent?
- ✓ Get a dog—but don't pick up the doodies.

The New York Survival Guide

- ✓ Give tourists the wrong directions.
- ✓ Have a favorite *New York Post* headline.
- ✓ Have a screaming argument with a stranger on the street
- ✓ Have a very strong opinion on the best slice (i.e. pizza) in the city.
- ✓ Know your way around uptown Manhattan.
- ✓ Make cars stop for you while at pedestrian crossings.
- ✓ Play dominoes outside.
- ✓ Refer to Manhattan as "The City" no matter where in the world you are.
- ✓ Root for the Mets and Jets.
- ✓ Sit on a stoop.
- ✓ Stand in line for brunch.
- ✓ Strongly consider acts of violence against your cable company.
- ✓ Survived a blackout.
- ✓ Walk fast everywhere, even when lost—check that—especially when lost.
- ✓ You've watched basketball at The Cage or Rucker Park.
- ✓ You've witnessed a person pleasuring themselves on a train.

The New York Survival Guide

Protocols for the Largest Ethnic Groups

The major nationalities you'll be exposed to in NYC are Dominican, Chinese, Indian, and Russian. This section will help you navigate their protocols.

Chinese
- ✓ Ethnic Make-up: Han Chinese 92%. The Han Dynasty is considered a classical period in Chinese civilization. As a result many Chinese began identifying themselves as "people of Han."
- ✓ Religions: Daoist (Taoist), Buddhist, Muslim 1%-2%, Christian 3%-4%
- ✓ Language: Mandarin is most common. Chinese languages are closely related but not mutually intelligible in spoken form, but they are often intelligible in written form. Chinese people will often communicate in their native tongue, while most other ethnics groups do not.
- ✓ "Face," is a combination of honor, reputation, and respect and is concerned with one's public deeds, respect for others, wisdom, and reputation. Chinese people act with decorum and avoid doing anything to cause someone public embarrassment. Disagreements are not aired publicly, but often met with silence. They are willing to subjugate their own feelings for the common good. Chinese people are very astute in

non-verbal communication forms, including posture and tone of voice. For example, frowning while someone else is speaking is a sign of disagreement, so that Chinese strive to maintain impassive expressions.

In public:

- ✓ Many Chinese will look downward when greeting someone.
- ✓ Chinese people will often take an English first name, as you would be expected to do if you were an expat in China.
- ✓ Do not offer cutting tools as gifts as they indicate the severing of the relationship.
- ✓ Do not give clocks, handkerchiefs, or flowers as these are associated with death.
- ✓ Do not wrap gifts in white, blue, or black paper.
- ✓ The word for "four" is nearly the same as "death" and should be avoided.
- ✓ Eight is the luckiest number, so giving eight of something brings luck to the recipient.
- ✓ Always present gifts with two hands.
- ✓ It is considered disrespectful to stare into another person's eyes.
- ✓ Gifts are not opened when received.
- ✓ Gifts may be refused three times before they are accepted.
- ✓ Gender bias is nonexistent in business situations.
- ✓ Chinese are non-confrontational.

Dining Etiquette:

- ✓ Chinese people prefer to entertain in public places rather than in their homes. If you are invited to their house, consider it a great honor.
- ✓ Business and pleasure don't mix.
- ✓ Learn to use chopsticks.
- ✓ Punctuality is a virtue, arriving late is an insult.
- ✓ Bring a small gift to the hostess.
- ✓ Remove your shoes before entering the house.
- ✓ Eat heartily to compliment your host.
- ✓ Try everything that is offered to you.
- ✓ Never take the last item from a serving tray.

- ✓ Chopsticks should be returned to the chopstick rest after every few bites.
- ✓ Hold the rice bowl close to your mouth while eating.
- ✓ Slurping or belching sounds indicates enjoyment.

Dominican

- ✓ Racial and economic issues determine social stratification in the Dominican Republic. The upper class are descended from the European settlers and have lighter skin than the lower class who are darker skinned and descended from African slaves or Haitians. Status is defined more by family background than by absolute wealth.

In Public:

- ✓ In Dominican society appearance is very important. People are fashion conscious and believe that clothes indicate social standing and success.
- ✓ Doing favors and collecting favors is an art form in this culture.
- ✓ Nepotism is considered as favorable due to family bonds.
- ✓ Trust is crucial to developing relationships.
- ✓ Respect is important, avoid anything to cause them a loss of face.
- ✓ Dominicans can be direct communicators and are not afraid to say what they feel.
- ✓ Small talk before a meeting establishes rapport.
- ✓ Dining Etiquette:
- ✓ Dominicans pride themselves on their hospitality.
- ✓ Give a firm handshake with direct eye contact and smile.
- ✓ Maintaining eye contact is crucial as it indicates interest.
- ✓ If invited to dinner bring chocolates or pastries.
- ✓ Avoid gifts that are black or purple.
- ✓ Guests are expected to arrive "fashionably late," 15–30 minutes.
- ✓ Always keep your hands visible at table, but no elbows on the table.
- ✓ Leave a small amount of food on your plate when you have finished eating.

Indian

- ✓ Religions: Hindu 81.3%, Muslim 12%, Christian 2.3%, Sikh 1.9%
- ✓ Language: Many Indian states have more than one official language. There are over 700 different languages, some of them not recognized by the central government. Although Hindi is the official language of the central government, Indian people generally use English to communicate with each other.

In Public:

- ✓ Indians are very conscious of social order and their status relative to other people. This from the traditional caste system. All relationships involve hierarchies, and people typically define themselves by the groups to which they belong rather than by their status as individuals.
- ✓ Religion, education, and social class all influence greetings in India.
- ✓ Men may shake hands with other men, and women may shake hands with other women; however, there are seldom handshakes between men and women because of religious beliefs.
- ✓ Indians do not like to use the word "no," because they consider it rude to not give someone what they ask for. To avoid disappointing, Indians may give a vaguely affirmative answer.
- ✓ Meetings will start with a great deal of getting-to-know-you talk.
- ✓ Indians are non-confrontational.
- ✓ If you lose your temper, you lose face with Indians.
- ✓ Indians revere titles such as Professor, Doctor and Engineer.

Dining Etiquette:

- ✓ There are diverse dietary restrictions in India, and these may affect the foods that are served. Hindus and Sikhs do not eat beef, and many are vegetarians. Muslims do not eat pork or drink alcohol. Lamb, chicken, and fish are the most commonly served main courses for non-vegetarian meals as they avoid the meat restrictions of the religious groups. Indians are quite happy to entertain at home or away.

The New York Survival Guide

- ✓ Indians are not always punctual.
- ✓ Take off your shoes before entering the house.
- ✓ Politely turn down the 1st offer of refreshments. The 2nd time say "yes."
- ✓ Indians believe that giving gifts eases the transition into the next life.
- ✓ It's the thought that counts, not the cost of the gift.
- ✓ Do not give white flowers as they are used at funerals.
- ✓ Yellow, green, and red are lucky colors for gift wrap.
- ✓ Gifts are not opened when received.
- ✓ Use your right hand to eat, whether you are using utensils or fingers.
- ✓ Finishing all your food means that you are still hungry.

Russian

- ✓ Ethnic Make-up: Russian 81.5%, Tatar 3.8%, Ukrainian 3%
- ✓ Religions: Russian Orthodox, Muslim
- ✓ Language:Over 81% speak Russian as their first and only language.
- ✓ Russian people are very proud. They accept that their lives are difficult and pride themselves on being able to flourish in conditions that others could not. They take great pride in their cultural heritage, so bone up on the Hermitage and what the Russians did to save it in WWII.

In public:

- ✓ Russians will often join a table of strangers rather than eat alone.
- ✓ They are notable busybodies and don't hesitate advising strangers.
- ✓ Men greet with very firm handshakes and direct eye contact.
- ✓ When female friends meet, they kiss on each the cheek three times.
- ✓ When close male friends meet, they bear hug.
- ✓ Do not give a baby gift until after the baby is born.
- ✓ Russian notice shoes, yours should be highly polished.
- ✓ It is best to err on the side of formality at first.
- ✓ Russians do not trust people who don't exchange pleasantries.

The New York Survival Guide

- ✓ Hierarchy is important they respect age, rank, and position.
- ✓ Russians see negotiations as a win-lose and compromise as weakness.
- ✓ Being asked for a favor means you have been accepted.
- ✓ Russians do not like being rushed.

Dining Etiquette:

- ✓ If you are invited to a Russian home for a meal, bring a small gift.
- ✓ Flowers are appreciated, but not "yellow." It means separation.
- ✓ Arrive on time.
- ✓ Remove your outdoor shoes.
- ✓ Dress well and in business attire.
- ✓ Russians often protest when offered a gift the first time.
- ✓ Offer to help the hostess with the preparation or clearing the table.
- ✓ Do not rest your elbows on the table. Hands should be visible at all times.
- ✓ It is polite to use bread to soak up gravy or sauce.
- ✓ Men pour drinks for women seated next to them.
- ✓ Leaving a small amount of food on your plate is proper.
- ✓ The guest of honor is the first to get up from the table.

You might be wondering. If there are 800 languages being spoke in NYC, where are the other 796 protocols? You're on your own for the rest. The easiest thing to do is stay in your pigeonhole where you don't need to worry about learning all this stuff. You can concentrate on other things, like whose name you're going to put on your Jets jersey.

While you consider that, here's a location guide to help you find the people you came to NYC to escape.

- Caribbean: Tremont and Wakefield in the Bronx.
- Albanian: Belmont, Bronx.
- Balkans: Morris Park and Ridgewood in Queens; Paterson, New Jersey.
- Caribbean: Hollis in Queens.

The New York Survival Guide

- Central America: Tremont in the Bronx.
- Chinese: Chinatown (where else!), Manhattan.
- Colombian: Elmhurst and Jackson Heights, Queens.
- Czech: South Slope, Brooklyn.
- Dominican: Corona, Queens and Washington Heights, Manhattan.
- Ecuadorian: Tremont, the Bronx.
- Egyptian: Astoria, Queens.
- Gay: Chelsea and the West Village in Manhattan.
- German: Gerritsen Beach in Brooklyn.
- Ghana: Highbridge and Morris Heights the Bronx.
- Greek: Astoria, Queens. Englewood Cliffs, New Jersey.
- Guyana: Tremont, the Bronx.
- Indian: Lower East Side, Manhattan. Jackson Heights, Queens. Iselin, Jersey City, Parsippany, Cherry Hill, New Jersey.
- Irish: Queens, Bronx and Spring Lake and Sea Girt and any other New Jersey town with three of more bars.
- Italian: Belmont, the Bronx. Bensonhurst, Brooklyn. Teterboro, Hammonton and Lyndhurst, and the rest of New Jersey.
- Jewish: Borough Park and Crown Heights, Brooklyn. Great Neck, Long Island. Rumson, Livingston and Lakewood, New Jersey.
- Korean: Koreatown, Manhattan. Sunnyside, Queens. Palisades Park, New Jersey.
- Lesbian: Park Slope, Brooklyn. (I'm serious—a guide actually listed this.)
- Mexican: Spanish Harlem, Manhattan. Passaic, New Jersey.
- Polish: Greenpoint, Brooklyn. Ridgewood, Queens.
- Portuguese: Iron Bound section Newark, New Jersey.
- Puerto Rican: Soundview, Bronx.
- Puerto Rican: Spanish Harlem, Manhattan. Williamsburg , Brooklyn.
- Russian: Brighton Beach, Brooklyn. Fair Lawn, New Jersey.
- Southeast Asian: University Heights, Bronx. Atlantic City and Camden, New Jersey.
- Taiwanese: Flushing, Queens.
- West Indian: Flatbush, Brooklyn. Jamaica, Queens.

The New York Survival Guide

Make sure your travel agent or website knows your ethnicity, surname, religion, and sexual preferences. Your neighbor will ask if you happen to run into him after the first five or ten years. Your ethnicity is only a starting point, however. Be prepared to answer: Who you voted for Red, Blue, or Blank. What religion: Catholic, Jewish or other. Are you a vegan, cross dresser, *Times* Crossword Puzzle Player? Everybody has a lable in NYC. Make sure you know yours.

Afterword

I hope you enjoyed "How to Not Get Yourself Killed" and that it helps your state of mind and gives you useful survival tips. If you have suggestions or comments, please let me know. It is sure to help others.

Thank you for your purchase, this entitles you to receive a free ebook as soon as they are available. If you enjoyed or hated this book, ask to be added to the launch list so you might badger me next time. If you have a book idea, let me know, I would love to collaborate.

Trick.Albright@gmail.com

About the Authors

Nigel (Trick) Roddey Albright is featured in Tim Heaton's series of Southern Gothic Techno-Thrillers. Trick is from Holly Springs, Mississippi, where his mother's family settled in 1830. Trick's father, Alistair, was an Englishman. In high school, the family moved to London, where Trick finished schooling at the Harrow School and the University of Cambridge. After a dozen or so years with an international hedge fund, and surviving a failed marriage, he returned to Holly Springs in semi-retirement to explore civilization's mysteries as they come his way. This is Trick's third book.

Buy Trick's books: **Let's Get Naked** and **Zombies Eat Last** on Amazon https://www.amazon.com/Trick-Albright/e/B083Y6184N%3Fref=dbs_a_mng_rwt_scns_share

Book reviews are golden for authors. If you enjoyed this book, please rate it on Amazon.

https://www.amazon.com/Tim-Heaton/e/B00TBEJ5V6%3Fref=dbs_a_mng_rwt_scns_share

Trick would love to hear from you: trick.albright@gmail.com

Tim Heaton is from Southaven, Mississippi, and is an Ole Miss and Boston University Alumnus. After a 25 year career on Wall Street, the markets decided he was a better writer than a trader. Tim writes on history, technology, and finance. He has lived in Santa Monica, Chicago, Memphis, Atlanta, Baltimore, New York, and London, England. Today, Tim lives in Morristown, NJ, where he is currently annoying his friends and family with tall tales from Dixie.

Please reach out to Tim, he loves fanmail tim.h.heaton.author@gmail.com

Tim's website has lots of fun Southern-themed tidbits: tim-h-heaton.com

Bibliography

According to a US News report, the 10 hardest working cities in America are Houston, Washington DC, Virginia Beach, Dallas, San Francisco, San Jose, Austin, Fort Worth, Arlington TX, and Seattle.

Graves, Jada. "The 10 Hardest Working Cities in America." *U.S. News and World Report*, August 7, 2013.

The most unhappy city in America is NYC.

"New York City is America's Unhappiest City: Study." *NBC New York* online. July 23, 2014. http://www.nbcnewyork.com/news/local/New-York-City-Unhappiest-City-America-Study-268228332.html.

Philadelphia ranked as ugliest U.S. city by *Travel and Leisure*.

"It's Always Ugly in Philadelphia." *NBC Philadelphia* online. October 8, 2009. https://www.nbcphiladelphia.com/news/local/its-always-ugly-in-philadelphia/2137628/.

The list of things that annoy expats are taken from several on-line sources.

McClear, Sheila M. "Heather Quinlan's Documentary Finds New York Accents Are More About Ethnicity than Areas." *New York Daily News*, May 13, 2013. https://www.nydailynews.com/lifestyle/documentary-nyc-accent-new-hearing-article-1.1340952.

The New York Survival Guide

From McClear's article:

"People think you're stupid," says Chiarelli. "I have a 4.0 GPA." But she is proud of her accent. "I would never try to change it," she says. [Alan] Dershowitz told Quinlan's camera that he never knew he had an accent until he was called on his first day at Yale Law — and everyone laughed.

New Yorkers tend to avoid speaking the dialect outside New York City.

'Negative' attitudes of other Americans may be influenced by the stereotype sometimes associated with New Yorkers: Gordon describes the stereotypical features of New Yorkers as "brash, boorish, criminal" and even "violent." Thus, the stereotype is anything but pleasant, which shows in the attitudes of outsiders towards New York City speech.

There is a big difference between the Pennsylvania accents, the Jersey accents, etc., etc. But I've been here for longer than most expats. Go to someone elsewhere for the linguistic truth. Other than the Locust Valley Lockjaw, it's too close for folks from other countries to call.

The constant use of the word "fuck" is unfortunately true in this area. I chose to use "f**k" because, like saying the word, printing the word is unnecessary.

Food.

Italian restaurants really do comprise around one-third of the restaurants in NYC. This fact was taken from the York City Department of Health and Mental Hygiene.

As luck would have it, an online reviewer actually did complain about not having a bread basket at Bâtard, one of New York's hottest restaurants.

The New York Survival Guide

The pollutants I listed are common in the Hudson and Delaware River. NYC and Jersey water comes from reservoirs and is safe to drink, but it usually requires conditioning because of the minerals found in it. The National Resources Defense Council has reported Philadelphia to be one of the "at risk" cities for drinking water.

The restaurant stories are just for fun. I heard one, and my wife heard the other. She's a Jersey girl who loves to grill the wait staff.

Greeting, insincerely

This may have been the most common complaint I heard from citizens of other countries. New Yorkers would ask, then ignore the answer. There are lots of articles and videos on the topic.

Catcalls will be frequent. Only thing you can do is ignore it. Andrea Peyser of the *New York Post* wrote, "A catcall isn't even close to sexual assault. Unsolicited compliments do not rise to the level of abuse, physical or psychological. Listen up, people—it is not a national emergency that women (and men) walking the streets of New York City may be forced to hear the words "sexy," "bless you, mami" and "damn girl!" uttered by strangers." See: https://ny-post.com/2014/10/31/a-catcall-crisis-thats-a-hoot/. True, but, in the author's opinion, it's another indication of third world civility.

A travel blog, PacSafe, reports that: New York City is often considered one of the worst cities in the United States for catcalling. We have a stereotypical image of a cab driver or construction worker making rude comments or noises, but catcalling spans age and economic status. In fact, catcalling has become such a widespread problem, that the NYC city council is considering establishing "no cat-call" zones around the city, making verbal sexual harassment illegal. Women are also putting their feet down in the Big Apple. A new app called "Hollaback!" allows women to take pictures of assailants and post warnings for other ladies around the city.

The New York Survival Guide

Booze

Several sources have data on the consumption of alcohol by state: http://www.thrillist.com/drink/nation/which-us-state-drinks-the-most-booziest-states

Don't drink the water. According to an assessment by Forbes.com, the colonial heart of America is the most toxic city in the country, followed by a pair of California cities, Bakersfield and Fresno, in that order. See more at: http://www.fairwarning.org/2011/03/philadelphia-named-americas-most-toxic-city/#sthash.4PQLGKnb.dpuf.

The particular state laws governing alcohol sales are correct.

Thrillist.com and others have similar lists on which bars to patronize. The bar scene changes even faster than the restaurant scene. There are about 3,000 bars in NYC, and there aren't nearly enough in Philadelphia to make it worth going there. Like restaurants, it's best to find a bar and become a regular.

The hangover cure from the *British Medical Journal* is true as well—and based on my firsthand knowledge of how the Brits drink—they should know.

Conversation

I make the observation that "Conversation is a highly evolved art form in the South." That is just my observation, but in West African conversation is an important part of the fabric of culture.

Most people would at least attempt to ignore a conversation they were in earshot of. To New Yorkers, it's an opportunity. You might be shocked to have strangers butt into conversations. Remain calm, keep quiet, they'll figure they've won and wander off.

From this excellent article by Deborah Tannen: http://www.pbs.org/speak/seatosea/american-varieties/newyorkcity/#tannen.

The New York Survival Guide

"Well-known author and sociolinguist Deborah Tannen explains why non-New Yorkers find Big Apple natives so pushy: It may have at least as much to do with their high-energy speech style as their personalities."

"New Yorkers have lots of ways of being friendly that put non-New Yorkers off, such as the interrogational style of asking questions. When we meet someone, we think it's nice to show interest by asking questions. Often, we ask 'machine-gun questions': fast, in a clipped form, and often thrown in right at the end of someone else's sentence, or even in the middle of it."

"People who are not from New York often complain that New Yorkers interrupt them. That's only because they start talking before you finish. So, who's interrupting? The New Yorker? Not necessarily. Who said only one person can talk at a time? Without waiting for a response from you they will ask: "How much do you pay for rent?" They may be sly about this at first and ask, "Where do you live?" What they are trying to find out is simply: "How much money do you make?" Hit the chute and tell'em how much you make!"

"New Yorkers believe that in a good conversation, more than one person is talking a lot of the time. New York listeners punctuate a speaker's talk with comments, reactions, questions (often asking for the very information that is obviously about to come). None of this makes the New York speaker stop. On the contrary, he talks even more—louder, faster—and has even more fun, because he doesn't feel he's in the conversation alone."

"A New York listener does a lot of talking. And if you like a story, or if you think someone has made a good point, you don't appreciate it in silence. You show your reaction fast and loud. This creates trouble when New Yorkers talk to non-New Yorkers. In conversations I taped, again and again the Californians and Midwesterners stopped dead in their vocal tracks when a New Yorker tried to encourage them by exclaiming, 'What!,' 'Wow!,' or 'Oh, God!' What was intended as a show of interest and appreciation sounded to the speaker like rude disbelief, or scared him into speechlessness."

"New Yorkers also think it's nice to let others in on their thoughts and tell about their personal experiences; the expectation is that others will do the same. Often, however, the others do not understand this unspoken arrangement." Or both are so busy talking that they don't notice.

"So, what's a New Yorker to do? You can try to change your conversational style, as some New Yorkers have tried to change their accents—and probably with a similarly patched-up effect. You can teach yourself to count to three after you think someone else has finished talking. This may work sometimes, although it may give you a belabored look when you're counting. But can you change your sense of irony, of the way to tell a story—even if you sit on your hands?"

I don't know. But in any case, don't feel guilty when you're accused of interrupting. In fact, you can complain, "Don't just sit there—interrupt me!"

The studies on New York speech and customs may be found here:
http://www.pbs.org/speak/seatosea/americanvarieties/newyorkcity/.

Online sources were used for the various urban guides. *The Guardian* was particularly useful for New York City. Philadelphia info was taken directly from http://www.discoverphl.com/outdoor-life/.

Demographics of New York City are verifiable from many government sources.

Tipping

The history of tipping may be found in several sources. An English attempt to abolish tipping in 1764 led to rioting. In the U.S., several laws against tipping have been defeated even though it would seem to be against the country's ideals and allowed for a clear servile class. By the last 20s, all the anti-tipping laws had been repealed.

All the facts about how people tip may be found in the many studies done of tipping. Studies also show that tips are based on whether the server was white, black, female, or attractive. I'm not sure how to use this information; it's just a factoid.

Always leave tips in cash, handing them directly to the person you are tipping, whenever feasible. This makes certain that the right person is rewarded and that the establishment, itself, cannot skim a portion of your tip by assessing the employee a percentage of what you tipped on the credit card. Many places are legally able to do this now. So, unless you absolutely need to charge the tip for business reasons, a cash tip is almost always better for the tip-ee. But the reason that servers prefer tips in cash is that they can avoid declaring the income on their tax returns.

Profile of the New Yorker

THE BIG SORT is the landmark story of how America came to be a country of swelling cultural division, economic separation, and political polarization.

Bishop, Bill. *The Big Sort: Why the Clustering of Like-Minded America is Tearing Us Apart*. Boston: Houghton Mifflin, 2008.

Sources for this chapter include:

http://donsnotes.com/nyc-nj/nj-cultural-map.html.

http://www.nj.com/news/index.ssf/2011/12/nj_man_puts_rednecks_hippies_a.html.

http://www.nyc.gov/ was the source for the Source Countries of the Foreign-born.

The influx of Germanic tribes into Roman society is one of the reasons given for the fall of the Roman Empire. They were not acclimated into Roman culture.

Source for business etiquette from various countries: http://www.ediplomat.com/np/cultural_etiquette/ce_in.htm.

Made in the USA
Columbia, SC
11 August 2024